Truth, Beauty and Other Realities

Ruth Eppler Wills

ISBN 978-1-957077-42-0

Cover design by Dori Larson

Publisher's Cataloging-in-Publication data

Names: Wills, Ruth Eppler, author.
Title: Truth , beauty and other realities / Ruth Eppler Wills.
Description: Includes bibliographical references. | Foxfield, CO: BBR Publishing, LLC, 2023.
Identifiers: ISBN: 978-1-957077-42-0
Subjects: LCSH Wills, Ruth Eppler. | Christian biography. | Christian life. | Spiritual biography. | BISAC BIOGRAPHY & AUTOBIOGRAPHY/ Personal Memoirs | BIOGRAPHY & AUTOBIOGRAPHY/ Religious
Classification: LCC BV4517 .W55 2023 | DDC 248.46--dc23

Published by BBR Publishing, LLC

Publishing assistance by BookCrafters, Parker, Colorado.
www.bookcrafters.net

Dedication

IN MY SOPHOMORE YEAR of college at Albion College in Michigan, my schedule was filled with classes needing additional laboratory time: German, Physics, Organic Chemistry and Botany. I was also in an English Literature class with Dr. Joseph James Irwin, professor of English and Journalism. We were to write a paper on a topic that interested us. I was interested in comparing the meanings of truth and beauty as both topics were meaningful for me. I never had the time then to think and write a paper with depth. What I handed in was quickly written and without depth. During these many years since that time, my interest in the meaning of truth and beauty has remained, and this book is the reflection of that interest. I thank Albion College for hiring professors like Dr. Irwin who required me to expand and search and continue to learn throughout my life.

Contents

Chapter One

Truth

QUESTIONING "WHAT IS TRUTH?" is something that all of us humans need to consider at some time in our lives. We begin life depending on adults and those around us, and what we begin to know is what we come to believe. As we live and grow, we experience more and more of life. We see, we hear, we experience, we begin making decisions on our own. These aspects of living then join together to become "our individual truth."

As an early teenager or younger we might begin questioning the beliefs of the adults around us; we might begin realizing that there are other beliefs and understandings; we might experience new ideas and possibilities due to the technological means that are available. How do we really know what is truth? As a young person, if we see something, then we tend to believe what we have seen. As we grow in understanding, we can begin to realize what we see is not always the truth or reality. Currently many young people believe what they see on social media. Is that the truth? Is that possibly someone who wants to persuade a young person it is the truth? How does one know for sure?

A definition from a *Merriam Webster Dictionary* for truth is: "1: TRUTHFULNESS, HONESTY 2: the real state of things: FACT 3: the body of real events or facts: ACTUALITY 4: a true or accepted statement or proposition 5: agreement with fact or reality: CORRECTNESS." What this statement says to me is that truth is something that is real, something that can be proved and something that actually exists.

I realize there are many ways to think of truth. Norman Geisler and Peter Bocchino wrote a book called *Unshakable Foundations** which delves into truth via logic, worldviews, science, the cosmos and the origin of life. Their discussions and writings involve a deep study of the subject of truth. There are many books from which to learn and study and discern for oneself what is truth. What I write about can only be what I understand, and my understanding of truth is that there are different levels of truth. The highest level which I call Absolute Truth would be things like the sun and moon, day and night, natural objects and living things that are around us that we see and experience. Also included within absolute truth items would be processes like gravity, elevations, weather, the way living organisms function and survive. A lower level of truth might be called Common Truth which might contain established rules of conduct or law, ways to establish and maintain one's health (physically, mentally, emotionally, financially), or following a current societal trend. The lowest level would be Individual Truth which is what humans come to believe due to their own living experiences.

People living in poverty and dealing with difficult living conditions have a much different experience of life, yet they can grasp and understand what is real for them. They know they are hungry, poor, hurting in many ways, and they have the intelligence and ability to see the absolute reality of the sun and moon, weather changes, and other natural forces. Within their community they experience rules and ways to deal with one another which is their common truth. Their individual truth is what is so unlike what many of us experience during our lives; for we might have abundantly filled grocery stores, various foods on our tables, beds to sleep on and medical help as needed.

Different cultures, ethnicities and heritages also determine what is one's individual truth.

Over the years many people have expressed their understanding of truth via their quotes in books and writings. Look over quotes listed by searches on the computer, there are hundreds and hundreds of quotes. Several of them I have chosen to share with you the reader. I really like the one by Mark Twain, "If you tell the truth, you don't have to remember anything." Another writer, Thomas Huxley, said "Learn what is true In order to do what is right." Then Andy Rooney wrote, "People will generally accept facts as truth only if the facts agree with what they already believe." Frank Lloyd Wright wrote, "The truth is more important than the facts." Many quotes deal with the idea of truth verse falsehood. Some quotes go much deeper. Ralph Waldo Emerson wrote "Truth is the property of no individual but is the treasure of all men." Fred Rogers said, "Discovering the truth about ourselves is a lifetime's work, but it's worth the effort." Albert Einstein wrote "The ideals which have always shone before me and filled me with joy are goodness, beauty, and truth." Finally, I wanted to share a quote from John Dryden who said, "Truth is the foundation of all knowledge and the cement of all societies."

My ethos is basically a belief in God who created the heavens and the earth and life forms in all their diversity. Because of this belief, I have read the biblical scriptures within various translations and wondered and meditated upon many of the words and thoughts that are written in those sixty-six books. One biblical quote that has haunted me for years is found in the Gospel of John. It is when Jesus is before the governor of Judea (the area where Jerusalem was located), and a discussion ensues which contains this question Pilate askes, "What is truth?" The whole dialog begins in verse 28 of chapter 18, between the Jews and Pilate, who is questioning the Jews about what charges they are bringing against Jesus. This verbal exchange including Jesus's response ends at John 18:38. The other three Gospels do not have this extended verbiage. Within the passage, Jesus admits He is a king of another kingdom that is not of this world. He says, *"You are right in saying I am a king. In fact, for this reason I was born, and for this I came into the world, to testify to the truth. Everyone on the side of truth listens to me."* (NIV) Pilate is caught between something he cannot understand and a people who can affect his livelihood. His choice was to protect his own livelihood and future. How do we respond to these words of Jesus today? Do we question or accept that perhaps Jesus is speaking of a truth beyond our understanding, a Transcendent Truth which is above the Individual, Common or Absolute Truths? "What is truth?" was an important question for Pilate, and it is still an important question today as we live in a time of faux copies of goods and false news.

Looking through the gospels, the word truth is mentioned many times. In the three synoptic gospels (Matthew, Mark and Luke), a phrase used 46 times is "I tell you the truth." In John the phrase used 25 times is *"Very Truly, I tell you."* During the prayer to his father concerning the disciples, Jesus says, *"Sanctify them in the truth; your word is truth. As you have sent me into the world, so I have sent them into the world. And for their sakes I sanctify myself, so that they also may be sanctified in truth."* John17:17-19.

I believe God is a transcendent truth. I read a passage in the devotional book *Disciplines* which also makes this assertion. On November 8, 2020 Garrit Dawson writes, "We are not the center of reality. The fundamental human choice is whether to acknowledge moment by moment that everything begins and ends with God. God's reality is as inflexible as gravity, as necessary as oxygen, and as dangerous and life-giving as the sun."* Mr. Dawson's comment about God's reality as dangerous and life-giving as the sun is a paradox that requires thoughtful and honest meditation.

In the travels of Moses while he was drawn to see a bush

which was burning but not consumed, Exodus 3:14 says, *"God said to Moses, 'I AM WHO I AM.'"* There was no questioning by Moses or can there be by us if we believe that God exists. Maybe we need a burning bush or a miraculous experience to begin to see or believe in the reality and truth of God. Looking at Psalm 119:105, *"Your word* (God's word) *is a lamp to my feet and a light to my path."* In Eugene Peterson's Bible translation this passage reads as: *"By your words I can see where I am going; they throw a beam of light on my dark path."* The light of God gives light to humanity in many ways for our lives: light of God is truth and God's truth gives inspiration (light) and freedom (lightening of the weight of life) and wisdom (enlightenment of knowledge) to humankind.

A prayer written by W. Paul Jones in *Disciplines, A Book of Daily Devotions*, is: "Lord, we are gifted with the power to sow truth everywhere, yet we contaminate the truth with mindless trivia. Forgive us when we seek society's noisiness instead of the quiet of your incessant presence. Amen."* As I finish this area on truth, my prayer for you is that these words might either support your beliefs or help you to sort out the meaning of truth.

Chapter Two

Beauty

IT HAS BEEN SAID that beauty is in the eye of the beholder. I am sure there are some things that one person will say is beautiful and another will say it is not. So, what is beauty? Sounds like my question in the first chapter, what is truth? *The American College Dictionary's* definition of beauty is: "1. that quality of any object of sense or thought whereby it excites an admiring pleasure; qualification of a high order for delighting the eye or the aesthetic, intellectual, or moral sense. 2. something beautiful. 3. a grace, charm, or pleasing excellence."

I can make a list of many things I see as beautiful, just as you can. What I seek to write about are areas of life where sometimes a thing within an area captures our attention, and we can exclaim "that is beautiful." These areas contain many small items, yet these small items may be of great meaning for the person experiencing them. For example, doing a caring act for another, seeing a work of inspiring art, or listening to a song that touches one's soul. A basic area for all of us is "nature" where beauty is seen in magnificent scenes, and in the smallest of scenes like a rain drop glistening in the sunlight on a spider's web. Nature has inspired peoples all over this planet not only with scenes of beauty, but also with the wonder of how and why which ignites and inspires questions in the mind. A third way that nature affects you and me, humanity, is giving us an experience of rightness and peace. As humans we exist gifted with three attributes: physical (our bodies with all five senses), soul (our intellect and emotions), spirit (a deep connection with our creator or beliefs). Nature can astound and delight our bodies, our souls, and our spirit.

Another area that can feed or support the body, soul and spirit is "silence." One may think that silence is not beautiful, only needed, appreciated, enjoyed or the opposite, unwanted, unappreciated, and certainly not enjoyed. Yet in this busy, noisy culture of today, there are times when silence is absolutely necessary for the sanity of an individual, a group, a people, and perhaps a nation. Silence can restore order by giving time to think and not just responding mindlessly. Silence can restore peace when bombarded by noise. Silence offers a chance to look deeper for the way to go, for the body, soul, and spirit to catch up to fast moving conversations and actions. Silence has been called "golden" – a term suggesting beauty. For many people a time of daily silence is almost required for their health, whether it be physical or mental or spiritual. Silence can be beautiful.

A third area where beauty can be found is "taking time to look beneath the surface" which can provide unexpected points of beauty. So often in our daily life we become so wrapped up in our thoughts and responsibilities, that we miss opportunities to look deeper. As we see others around us, we may be making quick judgements in our thoughts concerning how they look or act. If we take the time to look beneath the surface, we might experience another person's character and see something beautiful; a twinkle in their eye, a caring action or word given to another, or an insight of wisdom in their speech. Beauty can be found around us, but so often we are not looking for it or even aware that it might be found. We can be so introspective that we do not expect to see what is right in front of us.

Another and similar area where beauty is to be found is "when we lift up our heads" to see beyond where our feet are stepping. In today's culture with smart phones, it is a common observance to walk on a street and see person after person paying more attention to the device in their hand rather than lifting up their faces to see other people or anything around them. To lift up one's head is a physical action, but there is an emotional and spiritual result when one looks up from the ground. Being able to see more allows for sight to enlarge our attention, to engage with others or the environment around us which can change how we are thinking or feeling, or even help us connect to something greater than ourselves. If we do not look for beauty, we will miss many opportunities to see the beauty around us.

Perception is how we perceive or understand what we are seeing, hearing or sensing. Besides raising up our heads to see what is around us, are we "willing to take the time" to look at a situation in a different way? As we see drawings done creatively and artistically on the structures around us, can we reflect on the hands, the mind and the spirit that created that drawing? Do we see with negativity or with positivity? Do we make quick judgements in our living without thinking of other possibilities? Is there music or art, words or actions that touch our very soul and changes our attitude? Do we allow it to refresh our mental thoughts? As we read or hear another's story, do we seek to let it inspire our own narrative and open up new perspectives for us? As we look at the face of a loved one, does their smile touch something deep within us? Are we willing to see, hear or understand situations in a new way or are we blocked in by the framework in our brain? Can we open up a new window of possibility to see differently? Perhaps there is beauty to be found if we are willing to perceive life around us with a deeper expectation.

Perhaps these five areas can assist you as you are looking and longing for beauty in your life: nature, silence, taking time to look below the surface of life experiences, lifting up your eyes to look with an enlarged sight, and looking with a deepened expectation. In the book *The Walk*, author Richard Paul Evans, has a character who makes the following statement. "Ally, some people in this world have stopped looking for beauty, then wonder why their lives are so ugly. Don't be like them. The ability to appreciate beauty is of God. Especially in one another. Look for beauty in everyone you meet, and you'll find it. Everyone carries divinity within them. And everyone we meet has something to impart."* Those are powerful words filled with potential for how we live our lives. Being aware of the possibility of beauty can enrich our inner selves, our relationships with others, and our relationship with the creator of life.

Another quote that mentions beauty is by the revered American poet Walt Whitman, "Peace is always beautiful." Peace is what we humans long for. Peace to be who we want to be, what we want to do, where we want to go, and peace to live our lives. Peace for us as individuals, as a nation, and as a global covering. Yes, peace is beautiful. If we look for the beauty around us, perhaps a sense of peace may flow within us as well as helping us to move forward in a renewed way.

Chapter Three

Comparing Truth and Beauty

MY EARLY COLLEGE DESIRE to write of the connection between Truth and Beauty has not been something I have deeply thought about over all these years. At that time of life, I was so busy with other areas of my education, I was unable to commit the time to focus on writing. The years and experiences since college have provided many opportunities to challenge and deepen my thought processes. Now as I begin to focus on the connection between truth and beauty, I am finding a similarity and a dissimilarity between the two. There is truth to beauty and beauty in truth. As I ponder this, it seems like truth seems to be connected to an individual's understanding or objectivity, whereby beauty seems to be more closely connected to subjective feelings. Beautiful things are more universally shared by people than truths which are connected to an individual's belief. In other words, I am suggesting that perhaps: Truth is more objective while Beauty is more subjective, and Beauty is experienced more universally whereas Truth is experienced individually. Perhaps truth is sought with the mind and shared by thoughts, whereas beauty is appreciated by the soul and shown by the expression of response.

One's own individual truth is not always beautiful, maybe it seldom is, but one can often see beauty in common truths and almost always beauty can be seen in absolute truths. Common truths: rules on how we treat one another (with respect and honesty which produces order and security); health information and suggestions; societal interactions like education, arts, foods (production, shopping, preparation and sharing), churches, sports, and the list goes on.

Absolute truths contain: the universe, energy and gravity, nature and all the many varied forms that surround us, good versus evil in ways we respond to one another, hope, peace, joy and love. As one deepens one's thought processes, beauty can be seen in how scientific facts fit together, in the structure or intricacies of nature, and in the variety of humanity that lives around us. If we can see beauty in truth, can we acknowledge truth in the beauty that we see around us? As we see an unforgettable sunset, do we think of the truth that is shown before us? Is there possibly a creating power that transcends understanding? There is a reality about both truth and beauty, a positivity that we can perceive.

Thinking of the opposites of truth and beauty, I see negativity as the opposite of what brings joy to life. Lies and ugliness both can affect a person's initial response verbally, emotionally, and even spiritually. Negativity can quickly build and destroy. So often a small negative comment can fester in our souls and affect our living. A small positive comment can brighten our face momentarily and can be passed on to another by how we respond. I wonder why we as humans are more often caught up in the negatives rather than the positives. Why is it so easy to see the ugly rather than to look for the beauty? Do we also look for lies rather than the truth? Do we see truth in beauty? Do we see beauty in truth?

As we become older, one of the aspects of living that we often change is making our lives simpler. We have gathered "stuff" for years and begun to realize that some of that "stuff" we will never use or wish to keep. Clearing out our living abodes, our minds, our schedules, our relationships is a way for us to be more effective in our living. I love the word efficacious which means effective efficiency. That is how I want to live, being efficient in my effectiveness. Is there truth to that? Is there beauty in that? I think so. Simplicity affects our body, our souls and our spirits with a positive effect. Clutter, whether it is in things randomly scattered around our living space or relationships that do not encourage or support us, messes with how we feel about ourselves. I realize there are persons who deal with the need to acquire or possess: chances are they need professional help. I am not referring to those situations. I am only wondering about simplicity verses clutter which can form with over abundance. Life can be hard and keeping things in order can help us live in a more enjoyable way.

Truth and beauty can be found if we begin to look for the source of them. For me that source lies in an understanding of a creator who created with the mindset of organization and relationship. Baptist minister J. Dana Trent says "...we crave control—and we exercise it by relying on our own strength to create order. But this is not the nature of the revealed Ultimate Reality whom we worship. Our role as humans is to remain humble, trusting that God is powerful enough to create beauty from void and shalom from storm."*

There is so much depth that can be found in the meditation of these two words. Perhaps you will find time to think more deeply how Truth and Beauty are a part of your life.

Chapter Four

The Lectionary

EARLY CHRISTIANS ADOPTED Jewish customs of reading extracts of the Hebrew writings on the Sabbath. The first reading was from the Torah and the second reading was from the Prophets. Christians began adding portions of the Apostles writings as early as the years 50s and 60s A.D. According to the *NIV Study Bible*, the gospel of Matthew was written in the late 50s or early 60s and Mark was written in the 50s. Luke was written in between 59-63. There are differing opinions on when John's gospel was written, from the 50s to 85.* Paul in 64 A.D. writes to Timothy in his first letter, "*until I come, devote yourself to the public reading of Scripture...*" (1Timothy 4:13a). This practice of reading certain portions of the Bible has remained and enlarged to include scriptures from the Hebrew Bible and the New Testament.

The lectionary became a guide which enabled pastors and congregations to focus on particular scriptures throughout the whole Bible. Justin Martyn born about 114 A.D. wrote extensively on behalf of Christians. His First Apology, of two which he wrote, was written to the Roman Emperor Antoninus Pius who ruled Rome from 138 to 161. In Chapter 67 he writes, "*And on the day called Sunday, all who live in cities or in the country gather together in one place, and the memoirs of the apostles or the writings of the prophets are read, as long as time permits; then, when the reader has ceased, the president verbally instructs and exhorts to the imitation of these grand things."*

In the third and fourth centuries within the Roman Catholic Church, several systems of lessons were devised for churches in varied localities. The first attempt for a diocese to fix definite readings for special seasons during the year was made in the mid-fifth century. What is called The Historic Lectionary came around 471 and became the standard text for readings around Advent, Christmas, Lent and Easter. In the sixteenth century, the Reformation began in 1517 when Martin Luther posted his 95 Theses on the door of Wittenburg Cathedral protesting the Catholic doctrine of indulgences. During this time of reformation (1517-1648) some Reformers wanted to eliminate the use of lectionaries. Martin Luther (1483-1546) insisted that the historic lectionary continue to be used. For the next 400 years Lutherans, Roman Catholics, and Anglicans retained the historic lectionary as a basis for preaching, hymnody and devotional books. Over the centuries various lectionaries were used; one year and three-year versions were commonly used in worship.

In 1969, Vatican II publicized a new three-year series that supplemented the historic lectionary for the Roman Catholic Church. Then in 1970, the Protestant Episcopal Church, the Presbyterian and the United Church of Christ adopted the new Catholic three-year series as a basis for the lectionary in their churches.

In 1973 the ILCW, Inter-Lutheran Commission on Worship, published a new three-year series lectionary: Year A would focus on the Gospel of Matthew; Year B focused on Mark; Year C focused on Luke; and all years used scriptures from the Gospel of John. This lectionary used a reading of the Hebrew Bible as the first lesson and that reading coordinated with the gospel reading.

In 1975 an ecumenical group called Consultation on Common

Texts (CCT) prepared texts for use in North America and published the Common Lectionary in 1983. This version received criticism, so a revision was done and published in 1992 as the Revised Common Lectionary. This lectionary is the one that is officially used by the Episcopal Church, Presbyterians, United Church of Christ, United Methodist Church, Disciples of Christ, Lutherans and many others. This lectionary has four readings each week beginning on Sunday. The first two selections are from the Hebrew Bible or what many call the Old Testament. One selection from the books of history or the prophets and the next one from the Psalms: occasionally the first readings come from the book of Acts of the New Testament. The two selections from the New Testament are, first of all, the epistles and then the gospels. The only books of the entire 66 biblical books that are not included in the lectionary selections are Leviticus, 1 & 2 Chronicles, Ezra, Obadiah, Nahum, Zechariah, 2 Timothy, 2 & 3 John and Jude – 11 books.

The Revised Common Lectionary is designated by Advent in a lettered year (A, B, or C) and then Christmas is designated by the following letter, for example 2021 is Year B – Advent /Christmas Year C. This allows for the readings to go from Advent beginning in November and looking forward to the birth of Christ through an entire year of following Jesus from birth to end with the Reign of Christ in November. This is known as the Liturgical Calendar or the Christian Year.

Thinking and meditating through the various lectionary scriptures can take us on a journey of understanding God and God's holy Son Jesus. We move from Advent and expectation of a savior to Christmas and the birth of Jesus, to Epiphany with new insight, and to Baptism and the beginning of Jesus' teachings. Then three of the disciples are shown the Transfiguration which precedes Lent, Holy Passion Week, Easter, Ascension, Pentecost, and the Trinity. The first of November brings All Saints Day, Thanksgiving and the last Sunday before Advent is The Reign of Christ Sunday. Every year is a new year that we can move forward in our journey to know God and understand more fully the life lessons that can be learned by studying the Bible.

One might desire to read the Bible completely within one year, yet to begin to understand the scriptures and see connections between the various biblical books, following the Revised Common Lectionary (RCL) is a method to greater understanding of the depth of God's word. There are approximately 31,000 verses in the complete Bible. Using the RCL, one will read over a three-year period 6,000 different verses of the Bible. This is about 20% of the total biblical verses. Meditating and studying the content of a week's readings, helps to cement the Word of God into our lives. I encourage readers to try working through a devotional book on the lectionary for a year and experience the meditations, insights and wisdom from prominent Christians around the world.

Chapter Five

The Lord's Prayer

SO MANY THINGS have been written about this prayer, yet our understanding of the depth of its meaning can always be deepened. In that light I do have a few thoughts. The prayer, as I have heard and said over seventy years, has three general areas: a beginning doxology, a series of requests for our lives, and a final doxology. My thoughts have to do with the second and third areas.

After the first doxology, which means "a short hymn of praise to God" from the *Merriam-Webster Dictionary*, 1997, the requests begin with "Give us, forgive us, lead us and deliver us." Within the gospel scriptures, Matthew 6:9-13 and Luke 11:2-5, this is where the prayer ends. However, many religious communities add on a final doxology that echoes the ending of the beginning portion of praise, "For thine is the kingdom, the power and the glory for ever and ever, Amen."

In a first century manual of Christian instruction, called the Didache (Did-a-key), meaning "The Teaching" of the Apostles, there are rules and ways to live for young Christians. Within the eighth chapter of the sixteen chapters in that manual, are the words "for yours is the power and the glory forever." By the ninth century, "the Kingdom" was added to that phrase. The Didache was lost and then found in 1873 by a Greek Orthodox Bishop in

Asia Minor and published in 1880 into many languages. Over the centuries The Lord's Prayer, or known by Catholics as the Our Father, has been said by gathered peoples with and without this last doxology. During this time of research, I have come to realize that whether the people do or do not say the final doxology, the meaning of the prayer is the same for all denominations. For the Catholic and Orthodox churches, the final doxology is said by a priest who is their chosen apostolic successor. Then the Amen is said by congregation and priest. The entire prayer is shared and heard as a community and is known to be for all people who believe in God the Father of all. The difference between churches is how the prayer is said and who says what.

In the middle of the prayer a series of requests begin. First is for our daily bread which supplies life-giving means for living. While we often refer to bread as some form of food, it also might mean money that can buy food, or perhaps it can also mean that which gives us strength or the ability to live our lives. Reading in Mark 6:30-43 about Jesus feeding the people who were following him, they were hungry as it was mealtime. Thinking of the reason they were following Jesus to begin with, could be that they were hungry for emotional and spiritual food as well as for healing. We all need to be fed – physically, emotionally, and spiritually. Besides food and health for our physical bodies, what do we need mentally or emotionally? What do we need spiritually? What do we need today to help us in our life? Christ offers us the bread we need for the living of each day. Jesus says in John 6:35, "*I am the bread of life*." Do we believe that? Do we want that? Do we ask for that?

The second request is "forgive us out trespasses as we forgive those who trespass against us." That little two letter word "as" is so significant. Some denominations use the words "forgive us our debts as we forgive our debtors." Trespasses and debts, both are choices we have willfully made that might hurt another person. A different way of saying trespasses or debts perhaps is to just say sins. We all want to be forgiven of those things we do that hurt others, but we may not want to forgive another if they trespass against us or owe us a debt or sin against us. Giving forgiveness to another clears the air, allows further relationship with them, improves one's emotional state, and prevents hurt feelings from lingering and even festering into anger.

This prayer has given us a way to receive daily needs. It has then given us a way to live in peace with one another. Now as the third request is given "lead us not into temptation," those words give us a hint about who we humans are—we can be tempted. I do not think God leads us into temptation as much as how our own will can move us toward temptation. When temptation comes, our prayer can be, "lead me not into temptation, Lord." This is a way to guide us in the living of our daily lives. The fourth and final request is "deliver us from evil." This is to protect us from harm. Some may say there is no evil, only bad decisions. If Jesus says there is evil, I believe that evil is a real threat. The Bible is filed with messages of evil and goodness. A frequent lament in Psalms is the presence of evil enemies and the request to be delivered from their grasp. Literature throughout the ages has focused on good versus evil. Humans make decisions every day based on what they believe is true, or what they think is the right thing to do in a particular circumstance. For early Christians the Didache gave them ways to live and grow as a Christian. For us today, there are many resources to help us. This prayer by Jesus is filled with ways that can help us every day: daily needs, how to live, guidance, and protection.

Within these words, I find a connection to the last supper that Christ served with his disciples – bread and forgiveness. Jesus talks of bread as a representation of his body and a cup that represents his blood that is poured out for the forgiveness of sins. The Bible has many references of the word bread. One scripture that we may hear often is from Matthew 4:4 where Jesus responds to the tempter who challenges him to make stones turn into bread for food. Jesus's reply is *"One does not live by bread alone, but by every word that comes from the mouth of God."* Those words of Jesus come from the Hebrew scriptures Deuteronomy 8:3, where Moses tells the Israelites that God *"humbled you by letting you hunger, then by feeding you with manna, with which neither you nor your ancestors were acquainted, in order to make you understand that one does not live by bread alone, but by every word that comes from the mouth of the Lord."* Bread is more than just food to eat. If bread is the representation of the body of Christ, taking Communion will connect us to Christ physically, emotionally and spiritually. Remember what Jesus has done for you and be recharged, remotivated, empowered and enlivened to be Christ-like in the living of your life.

Thinking of the blood that flows through our bodies and its purpose of not only delivering oxygen but also taking away the waste products from each cell. Blood cleanses the cells allowing each cell to do its job in the body. Blood also protects against disease via antibodies that are produced within a certain type of cell when they are attacked by a disease-producing antigen. In the gospels, this Communion time is happening as a remembrance of Passover when the Israelites were protected from death by the blood of a sacrificed lamb smeared on the door frames of their dwellings as the final plague of death moved through Egypt.

In the sacred act of Communion, when Jesus talks about his flesh and blood, he is not speaking of the physical realm, but rather the spiritual realm. Today we do not see the physical Jesus, but we can envision him, hear his words anew and hopefully grasp the significance of his death and resurrection. As we take Communion elements, it is our body, soul and spirit that needs to be in connection with our Lord's body (the bread and the juice/wine), soul (his will for us), and spirit (his connection with the father). In that celebration and sacred time, we can be empowered and enabled to go forward renewed for living our lives as an extension of Christ in this world. Communion can be a time when we remember our loved ones who have died to this earthly life. Spiritually we might think of them present in that room as one of God's saints and be thankful for their influence on our life.

During Communion my mind is often activated around my relationship with God. The next few paragraphs are examples of those thoughts. One morning as I was thinking of connection with God, I wondered if my Jewish sisters and brothers felt a closer connection with God on a daily basis. I envy them if they do—with their meaningful Friday evening services and then on Saturday as their Sabbath where they focus on their relationship with God and God's commandments. As a United Methodist, taking Communion on the first Sunday of the month, sometimes the act or celebration of Communion is more meaningful than other times. Sometimes it is less meaningful and fulfilling for my spirit. Too often it is the later situation. I do not question my Christianity, I know I am a beloved child of God, and when I call on the Holy Spirit, I am very aware of help and strength. Yet there are times when I want more. A deeper and more felt connection; a greater sense of joy in living my daily life. I suspect this is true for my Jewish sisters and brothers also, maybe even some of the Orthodox faithful.

Currently taking Communion during the Covid-19 pandemic with the little cups that have the water on the lid. Looking forward to when we can have a piece of real bread. Remembering back to a service where the pastor encouraged the participants to take a huge piece from the offered bread loaf, saying there is always plenty of Christ's body to share. "Take a huge piece and be enlivened and blessed by our Savior for there is always plenty to go around." I guess I long for that to happen again, not just a little wafer or a small cut square of bread, but a generous offering of the representation of Christ.

Taking Communion today and using the little individual plastic cups that have both wafer and juice. I drink the juice and then realize I didn't get all of it. My thought was instantly, I need every single drop. I need the representation of Christ's blood for its cleansing power, for renewed energy, for the healing that comes through the freshness of the oxygenation which helps heal the body cells as it picks up the carbon dioxide and waste from the cells. I need Christ flowing through my body, my soul and my spirit.

During Communion this morning I heard the word "hungry" and began to think of our need to be hungry for the bread of life —physically, emotionally and spiritually. Do I hunger for Christ's presence? Do I cry out for help? As I read Psalm 42 and the words *"As a deer longs for flowing streams, so my soul longs for you, O God. My soul thirsts for God, for the living God,"* I realize that Communion is a time when my soul is hungry and longing for God.

I remember a time when I was helping to serve Communion within a large group of people, and I picked up a plate of bread and a cup of juice from the altar, handed the plate to my co-server and we stood in front of a forming line of people. The first person picked up a piece of bread and began to dunk it into the cup I held. With surprise and confusion, she said "the cup is empty." I had picked up the cup that was for show on the altar, so I quickly exchanged my cup for a filled one and continued to serve the people.

So often I think of the use of the word "cup" and how it represents life or an attitude. Are we half-filled or are we overflowing with joy, love, energy? Are we living a life with an empty cup? Is there something that is preventing me from experiencing the fullness that the Holy Spirit would give me? Is there something I need to get rid of? What do I need as nourishment? Do we really need a representation of the body and blood of Christ by bread and grape juice, if we can imagine what that cup contains and be in the presence of God's Spirit? What happens in areas where there is no wine or grape juice?

Maybe not even bread to represent Christ's body. What then? Is Christ's spirit not there? No! Christ is there and Christ nourishes the people.

During World War II when Dietrich Bonhoeffer, a German Lutheran pastor, spoke out against Adolf Hitler and the Nazis, he was imprisoned. While in prison, Bonhoeffer celebrated Communion with his fellow prisoners even when there were no elements. The focus is on connecting and communicating with God which can be done anywhere and anytime, even with an empty plate and cup. That information does not negate the importance of gathering together and in community, taking Communion with a congregation and dedicated priests, bishops, elders or pastors blessing the elements before serving them. We need to be with our Christians brothers and sisters. We need to be in community to help ignite the fire of God within us. Community helps to fan the flame of our understanding the love of God for each of us. Taking Communion with the community is a time to be praying for each one gathered. A time to remember the gifts of each person and how they have blessed one's own life. It is a time that the church community is strengthened and blessed.

Final thought around Communion is what our eyes will focus on as we begin a time of worship. Our eyes often see an altar with the particularly colored cloths of that season with beautifully displayed items; the Cross that signifies the death and suffering for our sin and the conquering of death to new life; the Bible as the inspired word of God; lit candles representing the light of the star at Jesus's birth, the light guiding the Israelites through the desert, the presence of light shown on Moses' face after being with God, the light at the transfiguration of Jesus, and a reminder to us of the light of Christ in our lives; flowers that remind us of new life and beauty. All of this on an altar. What we might not think about is that the altar is a form of a table, also an essence of Christianity. For a table is where Jesus communed with the disciples and shared the sacrament of Communion. He led them in a focus on bread and wine, signifying His own body and blood. During Communion is where we join our spirits with that of Christ as we remember the giving of His body and blood for us. Communion can happen at any table or no table, but the elements of physical bread or wafer and wine or grape juice can lead us into a spiritual connection with our Lord and Savior. It is also around a table where we connect with one another, family, friends, and guests. It is where we share what our loving God is doing in the world and right down to our individual lives.

In early methodism and even today a Love Feast can be held without a person to consecrate the elements. John Wesley first experienced the love-feast in 1737 in Savanna, Georgia. The practice had begun in 1727 by Moravians in Germany. This is a time when gathered Christians can share a bread substance and a drink while sharing scriptures, prayers, singing and focusing on the presence of the Holy Spirit. It is a great way to celebrate God in a retreat time.

The final doxology moves our prayer focus from our requests of God to who God is with that little word "for." Three areas of God's presence are listed: kingdom, power and glory. As I was hearing this prayer many years ago, I began to realize that God's kingdom must come first. Within God's kingdom, His power will be shown, and then the glory of God can shine forth. Today Christians speak of God's kingdom here on earth, but are we as Christians using our hands, feet and actions to bring God's kingdom around us? What does living in God's kingdom as a believer in God look like? Are we seeking to be transformed by the words of Jesus in the sermon on the mount (Matthew 5-7)? What about the power of God? As kingdom people do we expect God's power to work through us? Does glory shine through us as we seek to live our lives as a Christian? What does glory look like? If glory shines, then it is a form of light. Do our lives light up other people's lives? There is more work for you and me to do. Help us Holy Spirit to move and act with Your guidance.

The Lord's Prayer contains truth that we can see and read, beauty that touches our souls and spirits with praise to God, expectations of help from God, and peace for our lives. This prayer Jesus gave His disciples is as powerful today as it was when first uttered. Take some time to read and meditate on these words of life using the final doxology that brings our focus back to God.

Our Father in heaven
    hallowed be Your name,
    Your kingdom come,
    Your will be done,
      on earth as it is in heaven.
    Give us this day our daily bread.
    Forgive us our sins
      as we forgive those who sin against us.
    Lead us not into temptation,
      but deliver us from evil.
    For Thine is the kingdom, and the power
      and the glory forever and ever.
    Amen.

Chapter Six

Perfection

WHAT DOES PERFECTION MEAN? What does it mean to be perfect? Is there a desire within us to be seen as perfect? Is this a common thought for humanity? If this is a common thought, what might be the reason behind that thought? I wonder if it is to be accepted by those around us, to be accepted by our family, our school mates, by others just the way we are, then bullying, secret whispers, weird looks or motions directed toward us most likely would not negatively infect our self-image. If we doubt that acceptance by others, then our self-image is likely to be damaged and our thoughts might be "If we could be perfect, we would be o.k.!" Is that how we live? Does the desire to be perfect really begin because we see ourselves as imperfect, and we cannot accept ourselves? Is that why we want to be like someone else?

Thinking of our life journey and the little steps we take daily. We go uphill and downhill. We face metaphoric rivers that need to be crossed and the rushing waters of life push us away from where we long to go. There are easy times of straight roads and sunny days, or times of mud and obstacles and storms. Every day we seek to go forward, but sometimes we get on side roads or paths that take us backward.

Hanna Whitehall Smith's definition of perfect has always

helped me understand this journey. She writes about a tree and every point of growth is seen by God as perfect. The little buds, the new green leaves, the flowers, the beginning of fruit, and then the fully mature fruit are all perfect. As I am writing in the springtime and looking for the new buds on plants, I touch one of the lilac buds and feel its softness. I know it will mature into a leaf or a beautiful flower. My response is "How perfect is that!" Being perfect is a process, a journey. Each step forward is seen as perfect for its time. God sees us in all our problems and errors, all our pain and challenges and in all the times we take time to think of others and help them – that is love when we focus on another and not our self. God sees us as perfect for where we are, for God knows where we long to be and where God plans for us to be. I wonder if perfect is not the same as perfection: perfect has to do with a process while perfection has to do with a result.

If we think of how we do things, that is also a time where we desire to do perfectly whatever it might be. In my experience when I seek to have all things just right for a celebration or a job project or a gift or just a simple dinner for my family, the outcome may not be perfect, but is enjoyed and appreciated by the one or ones who receive what I have done. Perhaps then that project, or gift, or meal was just what was needed. Perhaps something is perfect when it works for the reason it was created: a tool made for a specific use, and it is the right size and weight and does the job well. Perfect is when something has accomplished a job and another person says, "That was just what was needed." How do we see perfection? Maybe perfection is not as big a deal as we make it. Maybe "being perfect" is not a realistic goal.

As a United Methodist member, I need to look back at what the founder of the Methodist Church, John Wesley said about "perfection." He sermonizes in two of his 141 sermons on this topic. In sermon #40 on *Christian Perfection** he talks about ways that Christians are not perfect and then ways that Christians are perfect. The ways we are not perfect are: 1-in our knowledge (we are not free from ignorance); 2-we are not free from mistakes or errors; 3-we are not free from infirmities (inward or outward) and thus not free from temptations. The ways we are perfect is only with the indwelling of the Holy Spirit. Wesley preaches on the first letter of John and the stages Christians go through from little children to young persons, to adults. He also preaches on sin and the cleansing from evil that is spoken in the books of the Gospel writers, Romans, James and other writings of Paul. Wesley speaks of Christian perfection as another term for holiness and that all mankind has the need to grow in grace and to daily advance in the knowledge and love of God.

In his sermon #76 *On Perfection** he preaches on Hebrews 6:1. "*Therefore let us go on toward perfection*...." Humanity does not have the perfection of angels or of Adam prior to his rebellion against God. The perfection mankind can attain is found in the word LOVE. Loving God and then one's neighbor, which is all of humanity, fulfills not only the Hebrew law and the prophets, but also the two commandments of the New Testament. As a human we cannot achieve perfection without loving like God. "Going on toward perfection" says to me that we are always in the process and never at the result of perfection in this earthly life. Wesley's sermon then focuses on other views of perfection: mind of Christ, undivided fruit of the spirt, putting on the new man, and being called holy.

If we begin to know how to have agape (Christ-like) love, we are on a journey towards God. One of the areas of learning to love is loving oneself. If we can begin to understand that the creator of all things good in this universe also knew each of us before we were born, can we then accept ourselves? Psalm 139 speaks of God knowing us even in the womb of our mother. God knew us as we were being formed; God knows us now in all our imperfections; and God continues to love us as we are. It is up to us to seek understanding and wisdom and to choose to be a believer that Jesus came to save us from our sin, our brokenness.

I once heard the little story of a person carrying two pails of water from a well to their home. One of the pails leaked and drops of water fell to the ground every time water was carried up the path. Later the person noticed that flowers were growing on only one side of the path. Wondering why there were flowers on that side, the person realized they always carried the leaking bucket on that side. Because of an imperfect bucket, something beautiful began. Perhaps it is through our brokenness, God's spirit can show forth blessings in another person's life.

What does that say about our expectation to be perfect? Does our understanding of "perfect" mean no blemish on our bodies? What about our thoughts, are they always without blemish? What about our spirits, how do they look to God? God loves us and knows us beyond any understanding we can perceive. Peace and joy are available to us now if we can keep our mind and actions focused on being believers in God.

CHARLES WESLEY, ca 1749* that captures his thought on perfectness.

This is the bond of perfectness
the anointing from above,
and all the law of life and peace
we find fulfilled in love.

Chapter Seven

Making Decisions

MAKING DECISIONS IS something we do every day. Sometimes the situation requires a new decision, but generally we face decision making on the same type of situation the same way time and time again. There are times when we make decisions because of what another person has said, or what one has seen or heard on TV/radio/phone, or what we might have read. How often do we take the time to pray or seek wisdom before we decide on a situation?

The Bible shares a time when the Israelites made a very costly decision. When what they knew took preference over a possible end to their wonderings is in the book of Numbers. This is the time of Moses in the years 1445-1405 B.C. Having crossed the Red Sea leaving the Egyptians behind, they travel three new moons and arrive in the wilderness of Sinai near the foot of Mt. Sinai. It is there that Moses meets God on the mountain top and hears all the instructions for his people as they move forward to the promised land. They are camped near Mt Sinai for over a year while Moses instructs the Israelites on how to relate to this powerful God by creating a tabernacle and the precious items for worship. The twelve clans are numbered and taught how they will move and camp in the coming days. The biblical book of Numbers covers this journey from beginning to end.

They have been taught a new way of living together with a focus on being obedient to God; they have heard the words of God through Moses; they have experienced the wrath of God; they have seen and experienced the power and protection of God; and they have seen what happens when they worship a false god. They are now ready to begin a new journey to the promised land. It only takes a matter of days to move from the area of Mt. Sinai before some of the people begin to complain that they only have manna to eat and not meat. God sends quail by the thousands near the camp and the people satisfy their longings for meat for over a month, but God's reaction to their complaint also brings condemnation to the people by a plague. The name of that area is Kibroth Hattaavah which means *graves of craving*. Miriam and Aaron also complain against their brother Moses which causes God's anger to make Miriam filled with leprosy. After a week of her being healed and purified, the Israelites continue their journey up to the wilderness of Paran which is near the southern area of Israel.

When they reach the wilderness of Paran, twelve clan leaders are sent as spies into the promised land of Canaan where they are to spend forty days checking out the land, the fruit of the land, and the people who live there. Retuning with a report, two spies report the land was favorable for them to occupy as God was with them, then the other ten spies report a land of good fruit but strong people in large, fortified cities. A decision needs to be made. As a people, their choice is to return to the wilderness rather than relying on God to lead them to success in this new land. God's response for this lack of trusting response is for each of the forty days of checking out the new land, the people will be back in the wilderness for forty years until all who voted against God would be dead.

Where the Israelites traveled for forty years is a triangular area in the Sinai Peninsula: the northern side of the triangle is about 150 miles in length; the depth of the triangle is about 150 miles from north to south. All in all there were approximately 1500 square miles with no rivers, and it is known as the wilderness of the wanderings. Geographically this is a place of baren rock and sand, mountains and cliffs, and not much vegetation. A Jewish word for wilderness is "midbar," and the root of that word is "davar" which is translated as "spoken word." During those forty years of traveling, they had to rely on God for food and water. They learned how God called them to worship, how to treat one another, when to stay and when to move, and how to trust God's Word. In this wilderness area between Mt Sinai and Kadesh-barnea, there are no rivers, but God provided their sustenance of water and food.

The place they had made their decision to not trust God and return into the wilderness area was at Kadesh-barnea. Reading in Psalm 29 the title of the psalm is *The Voice of God in a Great Storm*. In verses 8-9, the psalmist speaks of what happens when the Lord speaks and the wilderness of Kadesh is shaken. When we are in a wilderness time and do not know what to do, it is a time of confusion and indecision. It is a Kadesh time. It can feel like a great storm in our emotions and in our lives. We need to make a decision, and we are struggling. These are often times when decision making is filled with fear which can prevent us from making a rational decision. Perhaps we need to pray and ask for some Godly wisdom. Big decisions for us today often have chaotic thinking as we figure out where and how we are going forward. Bringing God via the Holy Spirit into the decision can help us to move forward and not retreat back into our own wilderness.

Wilderness times are not only times when decisions are to be made, but there are also possibilities that can be found and new understandings await us. Thinking back to when the Holy Spirit came upon Jesus, he was driven into the wilderness for a length of time before his decisions needed to be made. Wilderness times can strip away our comfort and what we rely on thereby opening us up for something new. Perhaps that might be the voice of God breaking through the indecision.

We are still God's people when we believe that Jesus is the Son of God, and God can make a way in our own wilderness. Isaiah 43:18-19 says *"Remember not the former things, nor consider the things of old. Behold, I am doing a new thing; now it springs forth, do you not perceive it? I will make a way in the wilderness and rivers in the desert."* (NIV)

Forty years passed and as the Israelites now prepare to cross over into the promised land, Moses addresses the people. Deuteronomy 30:19b-20a *"Choose life so that you and your descendants may live, loving the Lord your God, obeying him, and holding fast to him; for that means life to you and length of days...."* A later prophet, Hosea in the years 755-715 B.C. wrote in chapter 12, verse 6 about choices, saying, *"But as for you, return to your God, hold fast to love and justice, and wait continually for your God."* Do we hold fast to Jesus and his teachings when we are making decisions? Do we think and wait to make a good decision? Many times I need to admit that my thoughts are more on "me" and what I want or need. What does it mean to "hold fast" and how do we accomplish it? Perhaps by taking time to remember what has happened in the past, or time to think of other ways to respond, or thinking of "what would Jesus do," or maybe even a quick prayer for wisdom and understanding.

Chapter Eight

The Christian Year

WE OFTEN LEAD OUR LIVES depending on the calendar year, but I have found insight and wonder as I focus on the Christian Year which I wrote about in Chapter Four. How we live our lives may be the underlying question that is most relevant as we mature. Studying the Bible through the lens of finding answers for how Jesus and various biblical characters responded to the problems in their lives may help us to find examples and situations that correspond in some way to our own daily life. As Christians, we look to Jesus as our example, but the biblical narrative includes many characters from Genesis to Revelation that show ways people have lived godly and godless lives. We are all on a journey from birth to death. Every day we need to make choices. Every day is an opportunity to choose a new way to go. Maybe it is the same way we have been choosing, but maybe wisdom calls us to try another way. Being aware of new possibilities may be an answer to how we can deepen our relationship with our Creator.

Advent

The Christian year begins with Advent on the November or December Sunday after the celebration of Thanksgiving. Traditionally the themes for Advent are Hope, Joy, Love, and

Peace. Advent is a time of preparing for Christmas. We prepare our surroundings, our gift lists, our Christmas letters/cards, and even decide what special foods we will prepare. How often do we seek to prepare our souls and spirits? This time also brings decisions around gifting, financial worries, maybe even competitive energy with our neighbors. It is easy to get caught up in situations with negative energy, so we need to determine to take time each day to appreciate and be thankful for someone or something or some experience or even for oneself. These days during Advent are times of waiting to consider and pray and look within ourselves to find deeper meaning and understanding for our life. As we search for hope, we may find previously unfound joys that help us realize God's deep love for us. With a deeper understanding of hope, newly found joy and realization of God's unending love for us, we can recognize and experience peace. Hope, Joy, Love and Peace are all gifts to be found as we await the birth of a little baby called Jesus. Worship color is purple representing royalty.

The Christmas Season

This season begins with Christmas day and lasts for twelve days. It is a time for families to enjoy special music, beautifully decorated homes and store windows, colored lights all round, special ornaments, or decor from years past, cards and memories from friends, and perhaps a more friendly atmosphere wherever you go. This is a time to wonder about this baby Jesus, and the difference His life has made on us. Perhaps a time to reconsider who we are and our relationship with this newborn. Worship colors are white representing purity and gold representing divinity.

Christmas Eve. Live nativities and special services abound focusing on this baby Jesus and emphasizing the coming of light into the darkness that surrounds our lives.

Christmas Day. A time for family and friends to gather and celebrate the birth of Jesus. Perhaps attend a worship service, share gifts, eat wonderful foods and then eat some more. For me this past Christmas was like no other one I have ever experienced. Born into a large family, married and soon creating our own growing family, there has never been a Christmas celebration without all the joy and fun and work to provide a joyous family gathering. Sickness for both my husband and self this past year kept us from participating in decorating, gift searching, making cookies and preparing to host our family for Christmas Day. No caroling bells or beautiful lights or special ornaments or lighted tree. No special flowers or music or food. We were down to the essentials of what Christmas is about – the birth of a child called Jesus; the hope for the world who would save us from our sin. Praise God He has come!

Epiphany

Twelve days after Christmas Day, Epiphany begins on January 6th and ends on the Sunday before Ash Wednesday. Epiphany means revelation and commemorates the visit by the three Magi to see the newborn Jesus in Bethlehem of Judea. It reminds us that something new is to be understood, and we are called to be watchful. With the shining star that the Magi followed, the angels shining with God's glory in the night sky speaking of good news to the shepherds, light overcame the darkness. There are new understandings, insights and light–filled revelations for us if we turn our thoughts to why this baby was born. Worship color is green which represents growth.

Baptism of the Lord. We move from Jesus' birth to His baptism by John the Baptist, the authorization by God the Father's words, and the anointing of the Holy Spirit with the arrival of the dove. Here is when Jesus is driven into the wilderness for forty days followed by his confrontation with Satan. After this period,

Jesus' ministry begins. The Gospels write of Jesus's work in the countryside and the towns, the parables, the healings, and the feeding of the multitudes. Having shown the people miracles and healings, Jesus asks His disciples a question in the first three Gospels, "who do men say I am?"

The Transfiguration. Shortly after this question by Jesus, Peter, James and John are taken by Jesus up a high mountain where He is transfigured with a bright and glorious light, and a voice from the heavens announces that this is God's Son. We also are enlightened and changed when we have a Holy Spirit encounter. Something mystical happens and our lives are changed forever. The Sunday before Ash Wednesday is Transfiguration Sunday.

Lent

The Sunday of the week following Ash Wednesday is the first Sunday of Lent. The time from Ash Wednesday to Palm Sunday, which begins Holy Week, is forty-six days. Sundays are considered little resurrection days and a time to celebrate and feast. The other forty days are times of fasting with remembering and repenting our own sin and turning to cleanse our souls and renew our faith. Worship color is purple representing repentance.

Ash Wednesday. The burnt remains of the previous years' palm fronds turned to ashes are placed on one's forehead or on a hand signifying what is past is now gone, and there is something new to come. We are reminded of our mortality with the words that we are from dust and to dust we will return. As we look forward from our mortality to immortality with Christ, we seek during this Lenten time to change or improve how we live. Maybe we seek to not do something or seek to do something new. We desire to be renewed and closer in our journey of life to living as Christ would have us live.

Holy Week. This sacred week begins with Palm Sunday.

Palm branches were waved and placed on the road approaching Jerusalem as Jesus Who was riding on the back of a donkey entered Jerusalem. Palm branches represented a coming king for the Israelites, an end of Roman rule, and victory for their nation. Many cultures revered palm trees as a symbol for various items: victory, uprightness, fruitfulness, stability, peace, humility, sincerity and rest. Today in our Christian churches, on Palm Sunday palm branches are often waved by the children as they process into and around our sanctuaries during worship. We are to be reminded of Jesus Who is coming not as a physical king, but as the Son of God who can save us from our sins. We know that Jesus was a king beginning a new eternal kingdom for His father.

Maundy Thursday. "Maundy" means a command to love one another. As Christians, we remember the *last supper* of Jesus' life when He washed the feet of His disciples showing them that being humble as a servant is a way of respecting and loving one another. He speaks of bread and the cup of drink, first thanking God and then sharing that the bread represents His body, and the fruit of the vine represents His blood. Looking back to the book of Exodus when Moses led the Israelites out of Egypt, the people were asked to prepare for departure as the final plague was to come that evening. They were to prepare their *last supper* in Egypt by killing a sacrificial lamb and spreading some of its blood on their doorways. They were to eat the lamb's meat, unleavened bread and bitter herbs that evening. This act was called the Lord's Passover and saved the people from death as God's spirit moved over that land during the night killing all the first born of animals and man in Egypt. This first Passover occurred about the middle of the fourteenth century B.C. Our Jewish brothers and sisters remember what God has done and commemorate that time every year. They use unleavened bread which has no element that makes the bread rise. They leave an empty cup and an open door for Elijah, who is the forerunner of the Messiah or "he who will come." (Malachi 3:1 & 4:5)* That

Passover resulted in the saving of the Israelites from continued slavery to the Egyptians. What do we celebrate as the "pass over?" We call it Holy Communion, The Great Thanksgiving, or Eucharist. A time of remembering what the Father Almighty has done, and what Jesus has done by giving up His life to save you and me from our sin. Sin is around us all the time and brings death. Perhaps what passes over us and protects us is the power of the Holy Spirit. We now celebrate a sacred relationship with God, the Father, the Son and the Holy Spirit which saves us and cleanses us from sin. The Hebrew name of Jesus is Yeshua which means salvation. Themes for worship are portrayals of the last supper, Communion and washing of feet/hands, Judas' betrayal, Jesus praying in the Garden of Gethsemane, and the capture of Jesus.

Good Friday. As we think of the pain and process of crucifixion, how can we call this day Good? Jesus knew what was needed for His purpose to be accomplished. This is a day as we reflect on His death to look beyond the crucifixion and begin to understand and see that which keeps mankind imprisoned is now vanquished. We see Jesus speaking with compassion and not anger. We know this godly man is a good man Who can save us. This is good news – we can be reconciled to God and redeemed from the power of sin. Our mourning can change to rejoicing. The color for worship is black.

Holy Saturday. This day historically has been a special time to be baptized as a Christian. People know that celebrating Jesus' resurrection is coming early on the next day, and they want to be cleansed of sin and ready to celebrate resurrection. People also begin to gather for the next day's early morning hours, as they wait for the sunrise and worship services. They are waiting and watching for the new light of a new day—resurrection day.

Easter

Celebrating the resurrection of Jesus with worship services, special music, flowers and food. The words "He is risen" is shared with another, and the reply "Yes, He is risen indeed" echoes between Christians. The fifty days (50) between Easter and Pentecost can be a time of meditating and seeking to live as Easter people in our families, churches, and communities. Easter people are those who love God with all their heart, soul, and strength, and love their neighbor as themselves. Worship colors are again white and gold.

Ascension Day. Forty days after Easter, counting Easter and all Sundays, this day on a Thursday is remembered. Jesus was seen, heard and touched by the disciples immediately after His resurrection and for some time. Gospels Mathew, Mark and Luke all speak of seeing Jesus then ascend into the heavens. The Gospel of John's focus after the resurrection is the disciples' understanding more of who He is and the forgiveness of Peter by asking Him three times "Do you love me?" John's gospel shares what the purpose of John's writing is, "*But these are written so that you may come to believe that Jesus is the Messiah, the Son of God, and that through believing you may have life in his name.*" (20:31)

Pentecost

Ten days after Jesus's ascension, God's Spirit comes to the disciples baptizing them with the Holy Spirit. In the book of Acts, gospel writer Luke shares what happens when the Holy Spirit comes upon the disciples. They are enabled and empowered to witness to the truth that Jesus is the Son of God. The Holy Spirit came into the world to bless humanity with the presence and power of God. Because of Pentecost, today you and I are blessed and made able to minister to others. The Holy Spirit guides and empowers us to be Christ's presence in the world. Red is the color for worship on Pentecost Sunday representing flames of fire. Green representing growth is then used for most of the Sundays until Advent.

Trinity Sunday. One week after Pentecost, we celebrate that the Father Almighty, Jesus the Son and the Holy Spirit are the three in one, the trinity, our Creator, our Redeemer and our Sustainer.

Ordinary Time

"Ordinal" can mean counted or in order or refer ecclesiastically to divine service. This is a time from June to November that used to be called "Kingdomtide," or a time we as believers work at building up God's kingdom here on earth. How are we doing? There is much that each of us can do. Even a smile can brighten another's face. Maybe we are not witnessing about Christ with our words, but our actions and care for another can help others seek to know why we care. It is important to have a reason why we believe Jesus is the Christ, our Messiah, that can be shared quickly and easily – like an elevator speech, brief and succinct. This time represents our ordinary days of living and working and sharing with others.

World Communion Sunday. On the first Sunday of October, Communion is celebrated by Christians around the globe. We may use different breads and drink, but this day helps us realize and appreciate the unity of our belief in Jesus Christ around the world.

All Saints Day. The first day of November is the time to look back and remember our loved ones and all those who have nurtured us over the years. A time to remember the biblical characters who have helped us understand and grow. It is also a time to focus on praising God for loving us unconditionally and still calling us forward in being one of God's kingdom builders.

Thanksgiving Day. It is more than just eating a meal. It is thinking and giving thanks for what we have been given. Maybe we have family and friends to celebrate with, maybe we do not, but we can all have an attitude of thankfulness for our lives and for what is important for us.

Christ the King Sunday. This Sunday is the last Sunday of the Christian Year. When I first heard about this day, my soul responded with a strong "yes" Christ is King. I was delighted. Here was the answer to my spiritual journey. Christ is king at last. Do I live as He is king of my life every day? No, but I am growing in what I believe: God will overcome evil; Christ will conquer over Satan; and my life is secure in the hands of my Lord, Jesus the Christ. Every year there is the opportunity to grow deeper in our understanding and love for the Almighty triune God, and every Christ the King Sunday is a day to celebrate being in the kingdom of God, Christ's kingdom. As Christians we are called to be God's kingdom people every day of the year. When the stress and burdens of daily life come, I admit that often I do not remember to help bring God's kingdom into my situation. There is always time and room for drawing closer to God, and having awareness of being a kingdom builder which can help us make wise choices. Within Christ's reign there is hope fulfilled, joy resounds, love's source found and peace abounds.

Chapter Nine

Christ's Holy Church

WHAT HAS HAPPENED to the church? Why are so many different denominations losing their members over the past few decades here in America?

We have become a fractured church. Are we failing in sharing the Word of Christ? Surely this country is getting more and more in need of a refilling of God's spirit.

Maybe that is what we need, a revival or a Great Awakening again where the people realize their need for Godly help. There have been quite a few revivals in America that have occurred in individual places. There have also been three great awakenings where large areas of land involving many people have had revival.

> First Great Awakening, 1730-1740, Briton and the 13 colonies
>
> Second Great Awakening, 1820-1850s, America and England
>
> Third Great Awakening, 1875-85, Chicago
>
> Azura Street, 1906-1915, Los Angeles
>
> 20th Century, 1910-1970, Billy Graham

It appears our country and not just our churches is becoming more divided, and people are less interested in listening to one another to work together to find solutions.

Within my own United Methodist Church, members are frustrated, worried, and burdened down as our churches are challenged to make a choice between being a United Methodist Church, become an independent church or join with the newly formed Global Methodist Church. What do we believe? Which way is the way forward for us? Perhaps God is doing a new thing, a time of challenging Christians' hearts, and a time of deeper understandings of God's way. If people are being spiritually fed in a new way and turning to God, perhaps this country is being revived.

Seeing the Cross and Flame symbol of the UMC as I pass through towns, I smile and thank God for that presence. The symbol reminds me of Jesus and His sacrifice for me and the forgiveness of sin that is offered for me and all people who believe Jesus is the Son of God. The flame reminds me of the flames appearing near the disciples when the Holy Spirit descended upon them; the light of the star that led three Gentiles to a new king as a foundation for their lives; and the insight and provider of ability and courage that is available for me if I just ask. The Holy Spirt is present with us today and every day. Somedays we might need to "fan the flame" reminding and igniting ourselves to be attentive to God's Spirit. Somedays we just need to be quiet and listen and wait.

Christ's Church has done amazing work around the globe with hands and resources to help people in crisis. Mission work or "loving our neighbor" is being done daily by large and small churches of the various denominations. We are helping one another, but are we accomplishing the final words of Christ? The gospel of Mark in the sixteenth chapter, verse fifteen has Jesus saying, *"Go ye into all the world, and preach the gospel to every creature."* (KJ) Are we paying more attention to mission and not the message? The first commandment Moses and Jesus said is, *"You shall love the Lord your God with all your heart, soul and might."* (Matthew 22:37, Mark 12:29-30). How do we do that?

As I meditate on these words, our relationship with our Lord comes first and then the desire of our lives is to take action. Mark's first verbs of Jesus words to the disciples begin with "go" and "preach." Everyone can share thoughts and experiences with others that highlight the importance of Jesus, Lord, God in their life. It is not just ordained ministers who can preach, every believer can reach others with words that show God's agape love. Our world needs God's message and the ministry of God's love, so let us go with a message and with help by using our feet and hands and voices.

As I complete this chapter, I hear of a revival beginning in the southern area of our country. So many prayers have gone up over the recent years for our country. May this be a time of revival and may continued thanks and praise be given to our God!

Chapter Ten

Final Words

IN THIS TIME OF UNCERTAINTY and change, it may be time for us to reassess our thinking on how we are living our lives. What is your truth? Where do you find beauty? What is important for you? Is there "baggage" that pulls you down and keeps you locked within a particular way of thinking? Try taking some moments to focus on God and listen for any promptings. We all need to refresh at times. If this is a time for you to rethink and refresh and reconnect with God, my prayer is that you respond with praise and thanksgiving and action.

Often times we turn to our friends for a source of help and understanding, and they are very important assets for us, but there is a time when we need to look inward and find that source of goodness that is God. Whether you know that God loves you or not, the truth is God does love you with a passion and understanding that you will never understand. God has been, is, and always will be a mystery. Sometimes we want to box God in as a way to understand the who, how, when, what, and why of God, but the created can never fully understand the Creator.

Here are some steps to take when one is dealing with a bad day, hard times, depression or anxiety which is affecting one's outlook on life or attitude. Even a small step can improve one's attitude or how one is feeling on a particular day. Maybe one of these steps might help you improve your outlook.

- Be open to see or hear a new possibility or way of doing your work or living your everyday life.
- Slow down your breathing—take deeper breaths and let it exhale slowly.
- Be thankful for the little items in your life.
- Take time to do something that makes you happy.
- Take time to rest.
- Take a walk outside and look for a character in the clouds, or watch a bird or find a little flower growing in a strange place or just enjoy the breeze and the sunlight.
- Read a book you have been wanting to read.
- Write down what you are experiencing.
- Listen to soothing music.
- Think of something that makes you laugh.
- Try smiling—it might relax some of the mouth and forehead muscles.

There is goodness around us, but sometimes we are lost in the difficulties we face. Taking a small step can make a big difference in our attitude.

Journeys require little steps. The same is true of our life journey where we are learning to love not only ourselves, but others and finally the Creator of all living things. This Creator Who is the source of love. The psalmist in the 100th psalm writes of entering His gates with thanksgiving and into His courts with praise. Being in the presence of God requires both praise and thanksgiving.

Thanksgiving	**Praise**
Focus on oneself	Focus on another
Having received	Giving
A part of celebration	Praising God is a part of worship
Acknowledgement	Recognition
Using mouth and heart	Using all of oneself

Being thankful or appreciative for what is done for us is always a win/win for our relationships. It is like a smile that continues with those who receive one, and they may begin to smile at another person. Praising another person for doing a great job is always appreciated. No matter who we are, a word of acknowledgement or appreciation or admiration is a positive affirmation that we all need. Thankfulness and praise are both necessary in the living of our days.

I have prayed for the Holy Spirit's direction throughout the entire writing of this book, and I have prayed that you the reader will find some enlightenment or help along the way. I thank you for your time to read these words and to consider how God might be leading you at this time. You are a gift from God to all those around you and beyond.

Bibliography

Chapter One

   * Geisler, Norman L. and Bocchino, Peter, *Unshakable Foundations*, (Minneapolis, Bethany House Publishers, 2001)

   * W. Paul Jones, Disciplines, *A Book of Daily Devotions*, 2020, Page 234, (Upper Room Books need permission

   * Gerrit Dawson, *Disciplines, A book of Daily Devotions*, 2020, Page 374

Chapter Two

   * Quote from *The Walk*, (Book one of *The Walk* Series), Richard Paul Evans, Simon & Schuster Paperbacks, 2010, page 218.

Chapter Three

   * Quote from J. Dana Trent on page 17 of the 2021 *Disciplines*.

Chapter Four

   * *NIV Study Bible*, 10th Anniversary Edition, Copyright 1995 by The Zandervan Corporation, page 1431

   * Justin Martyr, *First Apology*, from Alexander Roberts and James Donaldson, eds. Ante-Nicene Fathers, Volume 1 (Buffalo, 1885). Public domain.

Chapter Six

   * *The Complete Sermons John Wesley*, Sermon #40 on page 215 and Sermon #76 on page 388. Published in the USA in 2013

* The United Methodist Hymnal, page 1, Copyright © 1989 The United Methodist Publishing House, Fourth Printing, 1990

Chapter Eight

* Celebrate the Feasts of the Old Testament in your own home or church, by Martha Zimmerman, Bethany Fellowship, Inc., 1981, Chapter 2 on Jewish Passover, pages 50-93. Great resource!

All Biblical references are from the NRSV, New Revised Standard Version, except those that are identified coming from a different version.

Acknowledgments

Writing a book is not solitary work. There are many people who have encouraged and supported me in this process. Their questions and their insights have inspired and enriched what I have written. I want to thank Rev. Laura Rainwater for her suggestions during my writing of Chapter Eight on the Christian Year. Rev. Tom Barlow corrected, suggested and inspired areas of my writing in the other nine chapters—thank you Tom. Daughter Dori's creativity in designing the book cover, and her enthusiastic encouragement throughout the writing process kept me moving forward. Without her, this book might not have been written. Thanks, Dori. Thanks again to Jan and Joe McDaniel of BookCrafters for all their help in the self-publishing process. Without the continual inspiration of God's Holy Spirit, my efforts would not have accomplished this work.